MARTIN LUTHER KING

THE PEACEFUL WARRIOR

MARTIN LUTHER KING

THE PEACEFUL WARRIOR

ED CLAYTON

illustrated by
DONALD BERMUDEZ

CANDLEWICK PRESS

First Candlewick Press edition 2017

Library of Congress Catalog Card Number 2017940754
ISBN 978-0-7636-7471-7

17 18 19 20 21 22 LEO 10 9 8 7 6 5 4 3 2 1

Printed in Heshan, Guangdong, China

This book was typeset in Caslon 540.
The illustrations were done in mixed media.

Candlewick Press
99 Dover Street
Somerville, Massachusetts 02144

visit us at www.candlewick.com

CONTENTS

FOREWORD

MY HUSBAND, Ed Clayton, had been employed for over twenty years as an editor for *Ebony* and *Jet* magazines when he received a telephone call from Dr. Martin Luther King Jr.

Dr. King told Ed that the Southern Christian Leadership Conference (SCLC) had a great need to hire someone to assist in the area of public relations, speech writing, press releases, and organizing press conferences. He wanted to interest Ed in joining the civil-rights organization and sharing his skills.

Ed had established himself as a prolific writer early in his career. He cut his journalistic teeth in Louisville, Kentucky, his hometown, where he worked as a reporter for the city's leading daily newspaper, the *Courier-Journal*. He started out writing obituaries, which taught him how to make a story newsworthy. He learned to report deaths—and lives—by using fresh words and distinctive descriptions.

Ed was later promoted to sports reporter, then moved on to work for Johnson Publishing, the renowned publisher of black magazines such as *Negro Digest, Ebony, Jet,* and *Tan*. As he moved up the journalistic career ladder, eventually settling in Los Angeles, Ed gained increased respect for his thoroughness, freshness, and accuracy. He was a reporter who knew a good story when he heard one.

After a lengthy telephone discussion, Dr. King

revealed that despite the SCLC's respect for Ed's talent, the organization was unable to match those skills with comparable compensation. Ed thanked Dr. King for his compliments but said that he could not afford to give up a lucrative job for little pay. Nevertheless, Ed was persuaded to go to Atlanta to discuss the SCLC's offer.

Ed traveled to Atlanta for a two-month trial period, during which he saw the vast need for his skills. He was so impressed with Dr. King's sincerity and the dedication and commitment of the staff that he reconsidered and decided to stay another two months before returning to his work in Los Angeles.

During that time, Ed met with Dr. King's wife, Coretta Scott King, who expressed a desire to do a benefit concert to raise funds for her husband's organization. She was a talented concert singer, having graduated from the New England

Conservatory. Ed agreed to help her launch the project, and he put forth a lot of energy planning and mapping her tour. He thought I might be interested in adding my own organizational skills to the project.

Ed was right. I talked with Mrs. King on the telephone from our Los Angeles home, and we spent countless hours discussing how I could be helpful to her. We launched the tour and, thanks to the support of several ministers who were already associated with the work of the SCLC, raised an impressive amount of money to further the great work led by her husband. She and I enjoyed the success and cemented a long friendship that lasted until the day she died. Our living friendship ended then, but my respect for what she did and the impact she made with her life remains today.

Ed's value at the SCLC increased rapidly

with the contributions he was making: organizing press conferences, preparing and releasing press statements, organizing photo files and setting up appropriate photo shoots, producing information pamphlets, writing speeches, and initiating many public relations print pieces.

As a result of monumental successes in such a short span of time, Dr. King and Mrs. King decided to ask both Ed and me to join their organization. They both expended time and energy to persuade us to move to Atlanta and continue the valuable service we had already rendered. After much soul-searching and deep thought, we agreed to the move.

My job was to travel with Mrs. King on her nationwide concert tours and also work in the office of the SCLC headquarters, acting in various capacities.

Over time, Ed realized that Dr. King's work

was vast, important, and valuable to the nation. He lamented the fact that not everyone was fully aware of this noted man's contributions to humanity and decided that a book on his life would do much to frame his good works for future generations. He especially felt that children should know more about Dr. King and his life's work and asked Dr. King's permission to do it.

Dr. King had been approached by several writers who had expressed interest in writing a book. He had politely refused all offers, but he said yes to Ed. Thus, *The Peaceful Warrior* was Ed's valiant attempt to preserve the life and legacy of this great human being.

The book, written in 1965, is as relevant today as it was then. Dr. King, founder and president of the SCLC, is considered the foremost advocate of the civil rights movement. He was thirty-nine years old when he died, and we are still remembering his voice and his vision nearly fifty years after his death. His name appears on streets, government buildings, schools, highways, housing projects, hospitals, community centers, and other public places, causing us to remember.

Dr. King was a visionary whose deeds greatly influenced the structure, texture, and tone of the society in which we live. He made equal rights his life's work, and although he was beaten and imprisoned, he never stopped teaching non-violence and making love his centerpiece.

I am fortunate to remember him as a personal friend.

Xernona Clayton

THE HARD WAY UP

SOMEDAY," whispered Martin Luther King Jr. to his mother as they sat together in church listening to a guest speaker, "I'm going to have *me* some big words like that."

Alberta King looked at her eleven-year-old son with quiet gentleness and pride. "I'm sure you will, son," she whispered back. And to herself she thought, *It will be a lot easier for him to come by* his *big words than it was for his father before him*.

She knew that if young Martin were called to

the work, he would very likely follow his father as pastor of Ebenezer Baptist Church. But, her husband, Martin Senior, had not had a ready-made berth to step into. He had *fought* for his place in the world, with sweat and raw determination.

Mrs. King mused on, only half hearing the rich voices of the choir. Her own father, the Reverend Adam Daniel Williams, had served as the pastor of Ebenezer Baptist Church for thirty-seven years. He had practically built it up from the ground. Martin Senior had taken over as pastor when his father-in-law had died, but he had had to take many giant steps first. Martin Senior was a sharecropper's son. He was born on a run-down farm in Stockbridge, Georgia, at the turn of the century—on December 19, 1899. Long before he had ever seen the inside of a schoolhouse, he was at work in the fields with his ten brothers and sisters, helping to plant and harvest their meager crops of cotton and corn. Until he was fifteen, he never had more than three months of schooling in any one year.

Even on school days Martin Senior had had his chores. He was up at dawn to curry, or brush down, the family's two mules. His schoolmates often teased him because they said he even smelled like a mule!

"I may *smell* like a mule," he once snapped back, "but I don't *think* like one!"

Martin's best subject was always arithmetic. Somehow it made the most sense to him and had more to do with his daily life than any other subjects. He often gave himself examples to work out that would not be found in his textbooks.

He would set himself problems like this to figure out: *Most of us, except Mama, work in the fields all day, every day, but Sunday. That's usually twelve of us. Now, if you took all those hours and multiplied them by the twelve of us, it would turn out a* lot *of hours. The boss,* he continued to himself, referring to the white man who owned their farm, *don't work half that time—yet he gets* half *of what twelve of us earn.* "That just don't make sense as arithmetic," he muttered to himself.

Martin's arithmetic stood the King family in good stead at harvest time one year. The boss was "doing the figuring" on the Kings' crop. Martin's father, James Albert King, was standing passively by. Mr. King could barely read and write, and he was respectful of the boss's knowledge of figures. When the boss had finished, he turned to Martin's father with a grin. "Well, we're all even," he said.

What the boss meant by "even" was that Mr. King's share of his cotton crop would be just enough to pay for the food and other supplies that the Kings had bought on credit at the boss's store during the past winter. Being even also meant that Mr. King would receive no cash for the long months of labor that he and his family had put into the crop. And there would be no hope of his receiving any cash for a whole year, until the next harvest. But Mr. King knew that, as surely as night follows day, he would be in debt again at the boss's store when they settled up next year. It seemed that no matter how hard all of them worked they never got ahead.

But this year it was to be different. Young Martin had been quietly observing the boss's figuring with an eagle eye. He did not quite have the courage to address a white man directly, but he said to his father, "Papa, the boss forgot to add in over seven and a half sacks of seed—and that amounts to almost a thousand dollars."

Even *half* a thousand dollars seemed like a fortune to the Kings. Martin smiled to himself. With all that money, he could see the whole

family going to church dressed in the finest. And wouldn't Mama be proud and pleased?

But the boss was not pleased. The boss had not *forgotten* the seed—he had merely conveniently overlooked it. "Just you remember," he threatened Martin, "I don't stand for no troublemakers. If you get uppity and forget your place, I'm going to run you off my land. Y'hear?"

Martin heard but he wasn't satisfied with what he heard. He was still working on his own kind of arithmetic. *How come,* he wondered, *we work all those hours and we live in a run-down, leaky old shack, and the boss works less and he lives in a big, fine house? Why is it that we always wind up with just about nothing?*

When Martin Senior was fifteen, he left the farm for good and went to Atlanta, twenty miles away, to find work. He could no longer stand the dragging, sad round of defeat and despair. He did not think that a week of backbreaking work for a few hours of forgetfulness in strong drink was a good way of life. It was his father's way. But it was not Martin's.

Martin was sure that more schooling would help him make a better life for himself, and that's what he set out to get. Of course, he had to work during the day to support himself, and the only jobs open to "Negroes" in those days were the hard jobs.

He hauled freight in a railroad yard and learned to stoke an engine. He was still a growing boy, and he pushed his strength to the utmost and beyond, every working day. The meals that he could afford didn't give him much to grow on, either.

At night he got cleaned up and put on his one neat, dark suit and went to school. Sometimes he could hardly stay awake in class. Many times he was so discouraged that he was almost ready to quit—but he didn't.

It took Martin Luther King Sr. eleven long years to work his way through high school, and he was twenty-six years old when he got his diploma.

Five years later, when he graduated from Morehouse College, he was already a minister, a husband, and a father, having married Alberta Williams when he was still in school. Their first child, Willie Christine ("Chris"), was born in Grandfather Williams's spacious twelve-room house on Auburn Avenue in Atlanta.

The Reverend King had come a long way from the run-down farm on which he was born.

THE GHETTO AND THE CHURCH

MARTIN LUTHER KING JR. was the middle child in his family. He was born on January 15, 1929, a year after his sister, Chris, and a year before his brother, A.D., whose full name was Alfred Daniel.

All of the King children were born in their grandfather Williams's house. In those days, there was not even the hope that black people might choose the neighborhood where they wanted to live. In cities and towns all over the United

States, black people could live only in the "colored section," or ghetto—a term that originally referred to walled cities within cities in Europe where Jews were forced to live.

Most of the Kings' neighbors on Auburn Avenue and the few adjacent streets that made up the Atlanta ghetto had only one thing in common—they were all black people. Some of them were uneducated field hands. When they came to Atlanta, they got the menial jobs only—as janitors or garbagemen. Some of them could not find steady work. Those who had never been taught a trade worked as day laborers when there were buildings to be built or ditches to be dug. When there was no work to be done, their families went hungry.

Some of the women were luckier than the men. They had been trained as house servants. They could always find jobs as cooks and maids in Atlanta's many prosperous white homes. Often the mother of a black family was able to earn more as a servant than her husband could earn as an unskilled laborer. These homes were restless and unhappy. Men felt they were supposed to provide for their families—not leave it up to their womenfolk.

But there were a few who prospered in the ghetto, too. There was a handful of college graduates. Most of them had entered the professions, being among the first black teachers, lawyers, doctors, and dentists. Like Martin's father, they had been strong enough to work their way up against terrible odds and everyone in the neighborhood was proud of them.

There were even some black-owned businesses on Auburn Avenue—a bank, two insurance companies, and a drugstore that grew into a chain of five drugstores throughout the city. In fact, there was a black man who was almost a millionaire on Auburn Avenue.

The heart of the Atlanta ghetto was centered on its churches. There were three of them within six blocks on Auburn Avenue. Ebenezer Baptist Church was Martin's family's church. Martin Junior was two when his grandfather, the pastor of the church, died while preparing his Sunday sermon. But the church remained in the family, with Martin's father taking over as pastor.

All the time that Martin was growing up, the church was his second home. Through it, he felt the heartbeat of his neighborhood. He heard his father preach a new way of life to his neighbors. The fiery young pastor begged his people to hold their heads high and not to take abuse from anyone, but always "to walk humbly with your God."

When their steps faltered and they were in need, Martin watched his mother and his grandmother pack baskets of food for them.

He grew up with the Bible and the words of Jesus as living things. He knew early what it meant to his neighbors to "turn the other cheek" and what it cost them to love their enemies or to "do unto others as you would have others do unto you."

By the time Martin was four, his clear, young voice was heard singing solos on Sunday mornings at Ebenezer. Soon other black congregations wanted to hear him, too, and his mother often took him to smaller churches in nearby towns to sing.

The tiny boy with his true, rich voice moved his hearers deeply. In the small towns where people had not yet learned quiet "city ways," the end of one of Martin's hymns was always greeted

with fervent shouts of "Amen" and "Praise the Lord." Many a small church almost rocked with joy after Martin sang. People clapped and "got the spirit," and sometimes Martin felt almost frightened by the noise. Services were much quieter at Ebenezer.

The people in the small-town churches showed their appreciation of Martin in another way, too. Often when he sang, the "thank offering," or collection, was a big one. And young as Martin was, he knew this was a good thing. Maybe some of the money would be added to the fund for a new church roof, or perhaps there would be children wearing new clothes when they started school—children who might have gone in rags if Martin had not sung.

SCHOOL DAYS

WHEN MARTIN'S BIG SISTER, Chris, turned six and started school, five-year-old Martin insisted that he was grown up enough to go, too. He was so passionate in his pleas that he finally convinced his mother to take him along.

Martin's mother was a schoolteacher and she recognized that her son was an exceptionally bright child, so she decided to enroll him in the first grade, hoping that he could pass as a six-year-old.

But Martin didn't remain in school long. Soon after he started, he let the secret of his real age slip out. He was telling the other children in his class about his most recent birthday party.

"And there were *five* candles on my cake," he said proudly. His teacher overheard him, and that was the end of Martin's schooling until the following year. But he hadn't been in school long before he was skipped ahead into his sister Chris's grade after all!

Soon after Martin started school, he began to spell out the signs in his neighborhood and around the city. One of the first things he learned to read was "For White Only." He seldom rode in streetcars or buses because his mother or father usually drove him in the family car, but when he did, there were still more signs to read. There was "Colored Seat from the Rear" and "Colored Exit by the Rear Door." Little by little, he was becoming more aware of what it meant to be a black person in the Deep South.

It was around this time that Martin began to notice a few rather special things about his father, the Reverend King.

One day as he and his father were driving downtown, they were stopped by a policeman. "Let's see your license, *boy*," the cop drawled to Martin's father. Like most southerners, the policeman addressed all black men, even venerable old men, with the belittling term "boy." The Reverend King reached for his license, but before he handed it to the policeman, he said, pointing to Martin, "He's a *boy*—I'm a *man*!"

Another time, his father took Martin downtown to buy him a pair of shoes. The white clerk came bustling over. He was courteous but firm: "I'd be glad to serve you if you'd sit in those seats at the back of the store," he said.

"Nothing wrong with these seats, thank you," Reverend King answered pleasantly. The clerk was embarrassed, but firmer: "But we don't serve *colored* in the front of the store," he tried to explain.

"If you don't serve colored in the front of the store, you don't serve *these* colored at all," said the Reverend King, and he took Martin by the hand and marched out.

Of course, things like this didn't come up every day of the week; sometimes months would go by without an incident. Martin spent a lot of time climbing the big oak tree in the yard next door, or sitting in its shade and reading. Sometimes he would fly a kite with his brother, A.D., or skate on the sidewalk in front of his house with Chris.

Every so often, there was a softball game in the vacant lot next door. One day, when they were playing baseball, Martin and A.D. were on opposite teams. Martin was catching for his team.

When it was A.D.'s turn at bat, he missed the ball, and the bat flew out of his hand and smashed into Martin, who was squatting behind home plate. There was a sickening thud, and Martin was knocked flat. He lay on the ground, pale and still.

"You OK?" A.D. kept asking his brother. After what seemed a long, long time, Martin sat up. "Sure, I'm OK," he said to his brother, "but you're not. That was your third strike — and you're OUT!"

One of Martin's roughest childhood experiences occurred when he was six. A white shopkeeper on Auburn Avenue told her two sons they could no longer play with Martin "because he's colored." The three boys had been firm friends, and Martin did not forget this.

Five years later, he still bore a deep scar from the incident. And one day, while shopping downtown with his mother, Martin had another bad experience. Usually, Martin liked to go shopping. He liked the hustle and bustle, and he especially liked seeing the toys and fine clothes in the downtown stores.

Suddenly, a white woman popped out of the crowd of shoppers. She planted herself directly in front of Martin and said the hate-filled word that Martin had always dreaded. "You're the little *nigger* who stepped on my foot," she bellowed. And before Martin could answer her, she lifted her hand and slapped his face — hard. Then she disappeared into the crowd again.

Like so many of his people before him, Martin was being taught about prejudice the hard way. He had looked the word up in the dictionary and found that it came from two Latin words — *prae,* before, and *judicium,* judgment. The definition said that prejudice was "an opinion without just grounds."

"The white lady," Martin told his mother, "certainly formed her opinion of me *without just grounds*!"

THINK BEFORE YOU ACT

MARTIN WAS SMALL for his age, and the big bullies looked upon him as a safe target. He soon found out that fighting back would get him nowhere. Still, he was not a coward and refused to run when he was challenged. So he learned to stand up for his rights by *talking* his way out of trouble.

Even A.D., who was a year younger, was a shade taller and more robust than his "big brother," and this rankled Martin. One day, A.D.

was teasing Chris. She begged him to stop and so did Martin. But A.D. kept right on teasing her.

Finally, Chris burst into tears. Without thinking, Martin picked up the telephone receiver and hit A.D. on the head. A.D. went out like a light and did not come to until several anxious moments had passed. A.D. developed an egg-size bump on his head of which he was very proud. But Martin did not like himself for days afterward because he had struck his brother.

Fairly often Martin seemed compelled to do things without thinking. Usually they were the kind of things that got him into trouble and made him feel guilty.

Martin and A.D. shared a bike, and Martin used to make his brother angry by taking very long turns with it. Sometimes he would disappear for a whole afternoon, and A.D. didn't think this was fair.

The boys had been forbidden to ride anywhere but on the sidewalk, and they had been cautioned to stay in their own neighborhood. But Martin just *had* to see what other neighborhoods looked like.

One spring day, Martin took a friend for a ride on the handlebars of his bike. They headed downtown to see what they could see. When they got into the crowded downtown section, Martin had a hard time dodging in and out among the pedestrians. He edged his bike off the sidewalk and into the traffic. Before he had gone a block, he was sideswiped by a truck. He and his rider were thrown from the bike, and the next thing Martin knew a neighbor was bending over him.

The boys and the mangled bike were brought home by the neighbor, who had been driving by when the accident occurred.

Both boys were badly shaken up and black

and blue all over. But, worst of all, Martin had to face A.D., who was pretty cross about the condition of *their* bike. *I've got to think things out better before I go ahead and do them*, Martin told himself.

Actually, Martin was always upset when he did anything that hurt anyone, particularly a member of his family. He was especially devoted to his mother, whom he always called "Mother-dear," and to his grandmother Jennie Williams, whom he called "Mama."

Often on Saturday nights, Martin's mother stayed up late to cook the family's Sunday dinner so that she could go to church with them the next day. Martin liked to stay up to help her. He would fire the furnace, or carry out the garbage, or maybe peel the potatoes. Sometimes he would just sit and talk to his mother, to keep her company while she worked.

His grandmother was a pleasant-faced,

cheerful woman, and Martin always enjoyed being around people who were pleasant and had kind words to say. When Martin's mother or father spanked him for disobedience, Mama's kind words would help to heal his hurt. Martin was Mrs. Williams's favorite grandchild, and she made no attempt to hide it. The two of them were very close.

One Sunday when Martin was twelve, the family had gone to church together as usual. After the service, Mrs. Williams had left them to go to another church, where she was to be the guest speaker at a woman's day program.

The rest of the family went home to dinner—except Martin. He sneaked off and headed downtown to see a parade, an activity that was strictly forbidden on the Lord's Day.

As Martin stood watching the parade, he saw a friend push his way through the crowd to reach him. The boy had been sent by the family. In a breathless rush of words, he told Martin that his grandmother was dead.

Mrs. Williams had suffered a heart attack at the church where she was to speak. She had been rushed to the hospital but had died before reaching it.

Martin felt that the judgment of God had been visited upon him because he had gone to a forbidden parade. He felt responsible for his grandmother's death.

When he got home, the family had already gathered to mourn and the house was filled with neighbors and church members who had come to console them.

Martin's eyes darted from one face to another. Reddened eyes stared back at him—accusingly, he thought. He looked for his mother, in whose face he hoped to find forgiveness. Finally his eyes met hers. Without saying a word, she buried her face in her handkerchief and wept.

Martin did not know what to do. *If only he hadn't gone to the parade!* He stumbled up the stairs. He knew only that he wanted to escape the accusing eyes. He had no plan when he threw open the rear window on the second floor. For a moment, he looked down at the peaceful, green quiet of the garden—and then he jumped!

When Martin picked himself up a few minutes later, he discovered that his bruises were minor. "Praise the Lord," he whispered.

The phrase reminded him of something way back in his experience. Yes, he had it! The small churches where he sang as a boy. He remembered hearing the swelling cries of "Praise the Lord" and "Amen" and the shouting of the

congregations that had frightened him. It was the lack of control that made him afraid then, and it was his own lack of control that he was facing now.

For a long while Martin sat on the grass, nursing his bruises and thinking very hard.

During the sad hours of his grandmother's burial, Martin contained his grief with quiet control. People said that he had grown up overnight.

THE DREAM BEGINS

EVEN THOUGH the Reverend King was able to make his sons' childhoods a lot easier than his had been, he never wanted his boys to be *soft*. He always insisted that if they wanted spending money, they had better work for it! And what was more, they had better do a good job, or answer to him.

Martin Junior began selling Atlanta's evening newspaper, the *Atlanta Journal,* as soon as he was big enough to lift the huge bundles of newspapers and to get a route of his own. He proved so responsible that by the time he was thirteen he had been promoted to assistant manager of one of the newspaper's neighborhood deposit stations.

One of the things Martin liked to do with the money he earned was buy books—special books. He had long since found out that the history books he was given in school had very little in them about "Negro" history, and he was determined to find out more about his own people.

After Martin finished the sixth grade, his parents sent him to a private "laboratory" school that was being conducted as an experiment by Atlanta University. The classes were small, and the students were given a great deal of individual attention by expert teachers who were eager to prove that black children could learn just as quickly as white children if they were given an equal opportunity.

Unfortunately, this fine school closed down two years after Martin enrolled. But he learned many things there that he had not even dreamed of as a public-school student.

He learned of the giants and the heroes among his own people—those who had fought for freedom and whose names were seldom mentioned in American history books.

He read of Harriet Tubman, the frail enslaved person who plotted and masterminded escape routes to the North for other runaway enslaved people, and of Nat Turner and Denmark Vesey, who led enslaved people in uprisings and rebellions against their cruel plantation masters. His imagination reeled when he read of Frederick Douglass and his lifelong fight to abolish slavery—Frederick Douglass, who was born enslaved and became a statesman.

He thought often of the fact that no effective laws had been passed to help black Americans since Abraham Lincoln issued the Emancipation Proclamation in 1863. Although the Supreme Court had handed down one decision that it was not legal for white children and black children to be separated, or segregated, in schools, he knew that there was still segregation in most of the schools in the South.

He knew that he would be proud to be like those heroes when he was a man. In his imagination, he could see himself as Nat Turner or Denmark Vesey, leading his brothers and sisters to freedom in the dead of night. Or he would dream that he stood on a platform and, like Frederick Douglass, made fiery speeches about a better life for black people.

The time had come for Martin to "get the big

words" that he once told his mother he would find someday. And get them he did. Martin learned to use his big words very well.

By the time Martin was a junior in high school, he was using his big words so well that he was chosen, along with several other students, to represent his school in an oratorical contest in Valdosta, Georgia. Making the trip with them was their speech teacher, Sarah Grace Bradley.

Martin did not win the contest, but he took second prize for his school.

On the way home, when the group boarded the bus for Atlanta, the students sat in whatever seats were vacant. A short distance up the road, however, more passengers got on the bus. Most of them were white people.

When the white passengers could not find seats, the bus driver turned around and ordered the black passengers, old and young alike, to stand so that the white people could sit down. Several of the older people began to get up, but Martin and the other students remained in their seats and ignored the driver.

This made the driver angry. He began shouting hate words at them. Still they didn't move. Then he threatened to call the police. The students kept sitting. Finally their teacher asked them to stand. At first, none of them moved. Then slowly, one by one, they stood. And they had to remain standing for most of the ninety miles back to Atlanta.

Miss Bradley feebly tried to explain to the students that she felt it was her duty to avoid trouble since she was responsible for them. They listened, but they were not convinced.

Yet, Martin wondered, *what else could she have done?*

THE CHOICE

MARTIN HAD MADE such giant strides at the laboratory school that he was able to skip the ninth and eleventh grades, so at fifteen he was ready to enter college.

When Martin entered Morehouse College in Atlanta as a freshman in 1944, this great institution was already more than seventy-five years old. Its founder was a black minister, the Reverend William Jefferson White, and it was supported by both black and white Baptists. Its students were all black people.

Morehouse was respected as a school that produced great men. Among its graduates were many presidents of historically black colleges and scores of doctors, lawyers, and teachers. Morehouse had graduated countless ministers, too — Martin's own father among them.

Everyone felt certain that Martin would follow his father into the ministry. The Reverend King took it for granted. But Martin was not sure. Above everything else, he wanted to choose a career in which he could help his people in the best way possible.

His mother sensed his indecision and suggested that Martin become a doctor. Maybe his mother was right, Martin thought. Perhaps he should become a doctor, as she wished. As a doctor, he would be able to help his people to lower the high rate of disease among them.

Or, what about being a lawyer? he wondered. As

a lawyer, he would have the opportunity to use his speaking skills to help his people have their day in court.

It was always like this. Martin could not commit himself to a career because he did not know which line of work would enable him to do his people the most good.

Even though Martin had not yet decided on a career, he chose sociology and English as his majors. Sociology would give him an understanding of the behavior of people, and English would help him become a better speaker—a good start toward *something*, he was sure.

In the end, it was an essay that helped Martin make up his mind—Henry David Thoreau's "Civil Disobedience."

Nearly one hundred years earlier, in Concord, Massachusetts, Thoreau had refused to cooperate with unjust laws. He had even gone to jail for what he thought was right. Thoreau felt that the poll tax law, which required him to pay for the right to vote, was unjust. So he did not pay his poll tax for six years but insisted upon his right to vote anyway. Then he was arrested and jailed.

Martin read and reread Thoreau's essay, and little by little he began to see that Thoreau's technique of civil disobedience might be used to help black people gain their rights. Why not simply refuse to obey laws that upheld the abuse and mistreatment of his community?

At last, Martin had hit on something that might help black Americans on the road toward freedom.

As the thought of civil disobedience took root in Martin's mind, he began to realize that he would have to try to get his ideas across to *many* black people if they were to succeed. Couldn't he best come before his people as a man of God, a minister? he wondered. A *new* kind of minister who would lead his people to freedom!

The more Martin thought about it, the more the idea of becoming a minister felt right to him. But he kept his decision to himself and prayed for guidance. He wanted to be absolutely sure that he had a vocation.

By this time, Martin was nearing the end of his junior year in college, and he still had to help pay for his senior year. That summer he joined A.D. and several of their friends and went to Simsbury, Connecticut, to work in the tobacco fields.

Martin knew that if a student was careful with what he earned, he could return home with as much as three or four hundred dollars to help toward his tuition. Working in Connecticut also gave Martin the chance to enjoy northern freedom. On weekends, he and A.D. went to town with their friends. They were free to go to any

movie theater or eat in any restaurant that they could afford.

The work, of course, was hard — picking and stripping the tobacco leaves on the seemingly endless stretches of farmland, day in and day out in the oppressive heat of a blistering sun.

When Martin returned to Atlanta, his mind was made up. He let it be known that he had been "called" to preach. Shortly after he entered the senior class at Morehouse, eighteen-year-old Martin was ordained as a minister and elected assistant pastor of Ebenezer Baptist Church.

It was a jubilant day for everyone — particularly Martin's father.

GETTING READY

NOW IT WAS CLEAR to Martin where he wanted to go. His interest in religion was beginning to take on new meaning. His passion for philosophy, fired by the writings of Thoreau, led him to a constant and exciting search for other writers and philosophers. These, he believed, would supply him with the additional knowledge that he needed to fight injustice.

In June 1948, Martin graduated from Morehouse College, but he did not yet feel that he had enough education to be the kind of minister that he wanted to be. So he took advantage of the scholarship he had been awarded and decided to enter Crozer Theological Seminary in Chester, Pennsylvania.

Now Martin would *really* be on his own. This would not be like going to college at Morehouse, where he had divided his time between school and home. At Crozer, he would be living in the North, six hundred miles away from home — and competing with white students.

He began feeling a new sense of adulthood and personal responsibility. He would be one of six black people in a student body of about a hundred. He knew that in a sense he would always be on exhibit, and he was determined that no action of his would ever let his people down.

Making friends always had been easy for Martin, and Crozer was a friendly place. But there was one white student from North Carolina who seemed unwilling to accept black students as his classmates. When referring to a black person, he often used the insulting term *darkie*.

Martin did not become fully aware of how the student from North Carolina felt toward black people until he became involved in an incident with him. It grew out of a prank. Whenever a group of them found another student out of his room, they would go in and tear the room up. They upended his desk and chairs and made such a shambles of the room that it would take several hours to clean up the mess.

The student from North Carolina had joined in the fun several times, but one day he returned to find his own room had received the treatment. Immediately he went to Martin and accused him of having done the job out of spite. Then he pulled out a gun and threatened to shoot Martin.

Calmly, Martin denied that he had even been in the group that had overturned the room. By now, fellow students had begun gathering around the two and the student from North Carolina was persuaded to put down his gun.

But the matter did not end there. It was brought before both the student government board and the faculty. Martin refused to press charges. Finally the student admitted that he had been in the wrong and publicly apologized. In later years he and Martin became very good friends.

At Crozer, much of Martin's study was devoted to the teachings of Jesus and to the writings of other great leaders of all faiths. He became acquainted with the life and teachings of the gentle leader of India, Mohandas K. Gandhi, who had been able to free his people from British oppression with nonviolent methods.

Like Thoreau, Gandhi rebelled against laws that he considered unjust. But Gandhi went further than Thoreau. He taught his followers to break laws that seemed harsh and unjust, to allow themselves to be arrested, and to accept the clubbings of the police without running away or striking back. He taught love for the oppressor—not hate.

Here, at last, Martin realized, was the long-awaited method to deal with the unjust laws that kept black Americans only half-free.

Why not combine the teachings and ideas of Jesus Christ, Thoreau, and Gandhi? Martin asked himself. Hadn't Jesus said, "Love your enemies"? Hadn't Thoreau and Gandhi rebelled against unjust laws? And hadn't Gandhi already shown that love had helped to end persecution for an entire nation?

Martin's mind reeled with the possibilities of such a method. It could work. He *knew* it could.

But how to get it across? Where? When?

It would not be easy to bring this new idea to the black community.

He would just have to be patient and wait for the right moment.

THE DREAM UNFOLDS

THE THREE YEARS at Crozer slipped past quickly. Living in the North most of each year gave Martin a chance to know white people who were on his side. But Martin also discovered prejudice in the North. There were no "For White Only" signs, but some places still did not welcome black people, despite laws that said they must be served.

Martin graduated from Crozer at twenty-two. He was at the head of his class and gave the valedictory address. He also received other honors, among them the Lewis Crozer Fellowship award of $1,200. This money was to be applied to two more years of study at the school of his choice. Now Martin would be able to attain the highest degree in education: a doctorate.

Martin chose Boston University and rented a room in the city. He drove back and forth to school in the green Chevrolet his parents gave him as a graduation present.

It was in Boston that Martin met the lovely Coretta Scott, who was studying voice at the New England Conservatory of Music. Like Martin, she too was from the South and had also known the whiplash of prejudice. Before their first date was over, Martin was hinting about marriage, even though they each had a year more of schooling ahead of them.

As the months passed, Martin's talk of

marriage became more pressing. Coretta did not know what to do. She wanted to become a concert singer and had hoped not to marry until her career was safely launched.

Martin, however, convinced her otherwise, and they were married on June 18, 1953. The ceremony was performed by Martin's father in the garden of Coretta's home.

By the time the newlyweds had completed their last year of school, they were faced with a very serious decision. The new Dr. King had offers of teaching jobs at three colleges. Also, there were three churches, two of them in the North, that wanted Dr. King as their pastor. The third church was in the South — in Montgomery, Alabama.

Both Dr. King and his wife were tempted to turn their backs on the South, where they both had suffered as second-class citizens. They knew

that by accepting one of the offers in the North, they could lead an easier life.

Yet the South, despite its mistreatment of black people, was still "home." It was where their roots were, and Martin and Coretta wanted to be back with their family and friends.

Martin accepted the pastorate of the Dexter Avenue Baptist Church in Montgomery. Together the young couple hoped to help in shaping a brighter future for their people.

THE SPARK CATCHES

MARTIN'S FATHER had objected to his decision to accept the pastorate of Dexter Avenue Baptist Church. He had hoped that Martin would return to Atlanta and become co-pastor of Ebenezer, but he had other reasons, too.

Reverend King remembered that on one visit to Montgomery many years before, he and a group of ministers had boarded a trolley. The white conductor had taken their fares at the front end and then ordered them to get off the trolley and board it again at the "Negro" entrance in the back. Reverend King had refused to do this, demanding his money back. He stood his ground, and a heated argument followed. Finally his friends persuaded him to get off the trolley.

Things had not changed much when his son arrived in Montgomery twenty-five years later. Buses had replaced the trolley cars, but black passengers still had to take their seats in the rear.

In his Sunday sermons, Martin Junior—Dr. King—was soon speaking out plainly against such injustices. He had also started talking to other ministers and to black leaders in the community about Gandhi's program of civil disobedience.

Why couldn't such a plan work in Montgomery? he wondered. "What would happen if black people stopped riding the buses as a protest?" he asked his friends. They thought that such a plan might work *someday*.

Then one day, after Dr. King had been in Montgomery over a year, and there was still only talk in the black community about "doing something" to help themselves, a middle-aged seamstress, Rosa Parks, *did something*. After work, she boarded a bus in downtown Montgomery, paid her fare, and took the first seat behind a sign reading "Reserved for White." Three other black passengers also sat near her in the white section.

As the bus began to fill up with white passengers, the driver ordered the black people to stand and make room for them. The other three black passengers promptly gave up their seats. Mrs. Parks remained in hers.

Again the driver ordered her to stand. She remained in her seat. A policeman was called, and Mrs. Parks was arrested and taken to jail. It was Thursday evening, December 1, 1955.

One of the first people to hear of Mrs. Parks's arrest was E. D. Nixon, who worked as a Pullman porter—a railway baggage handler. Nixon once had been state president of the National Association for the Advancement of Colored People (NAACP), the oldest black civil-rights group. Mrs. Parks had been his secretary. When he was notified of her arrest, he immediately went to sign the bond for her release.

Mrs. Parks's arrest troubled Mr. Nixon deeply. He felt that it was an outrage against the black community. Early the next morning, Mr. Nixon called Dr. King and suggested that black people stop riding the buses as a protest against Mrs. Parks's arrest. Dr. King agreed that the time to boycott the buses had come.

That night, a meeting of black leaders was held in Dr. King's church. The ministers who were present agreed to speak to their congregations on Sunday about the tremendous importance of their refusing to ride the buses.

The group also planned to print and distribute seven thousand leaflets, notifying the black community of the bus boycott.

The white community soon learned of the boycott, too. A black maid was given one of the leaflets and, being unable to read, she asked her employer to read it to her. The white woman could hardly believe what she was reading—how *dared* they? Outraged, she called a newspaper.

By Saturday morning, the planned boycott was on the front page of the newspaper. Dr. King and his associates were delighted—a white publication was giving them far better distribution than they had planned. The leaflet's message was included in the article.

DON'T RIDE THE BUS
to work, to town, to school, or any place
Monday, December 5....
If you work, take a cab, or share a ride, or walk.
Come to a mass meeting, Monday at 7:00 p.m.,
at the Holt Street Baptist Church
for further instruction.

When Monday morning finally came, Martin and his wife were up by 5:30 a.m. to see how effective the boycott would be. The bus line that went past their home was used by more black passengers than any other line. It was usually crowded with domestic workers in the early morning.

As they watched from a front window, they saw the first bus roll slowly by. It was empty! Fifteen minutes later, a second bus came by. It, too, was empty. The third bus carried only two *white* passengers.

Dr. King dressed hurriedly and rushed out of the house to his car. For more than an hour, he cruised around, observing every bus. He counted only eight black passengers. On any normal day, the buses would have been carrying some 17,500 black workers to and from their jobs.

WALKING FOR FREEDOM

MRS. PARKS WAS FINED ten dollars and court costs for disobeying the city's segregation law, which did not grant black people the same rights as white people. Now, for the first time, there was a clear-cut test case to challenge the unjust segregation laws.

Later that afternoon, at a meeting of boycott leaders, Dr. King was unanimously elected president of a newly formed organization, the Montgomery Improvement Association. This group was to set policy and plan strategy for the boycott.

Returning home that evening for a few moments before the mass meeting, Dr. King told his wife that he was deeply concerned about the new responsibility that suddenly had been thrust upon him. He explained that he would no longer have much time to spend at home with her and with their two-week-old daughter, Yolanda. "And," he finished in a quiet voice, "it is only fair to warn you that there is an element of danger in all this."

Coretta listened calmly to all Martin had to say. Finally, in a reassuring voice, she said, "Whatever you do, you know you have my backing." Then she added, "We'll worry about danger when we're in it," and managed a half-smile.

At the mass meeting that night, the Holt Street Church was filled to overflowing and about three thousand more people were unable to get in. Loudspeakers were set up outside so that they could hear what was being said inside the church.

With unusual fervor and spiritual outpouring, the huge crowd lifted its voice in the opening hymn. With one mighty voice came the words "Onward, Christian soldiers . . ." Then Dr. King rose to speak and the crowd was silent. The television cameras began to roll—the bus boycott had become news.

"We are here this evening for serious business," Dr. King said in his clear, strong voice. "We are here in a general sense because first and foremost we are American citizens and we are determined to apply our citizenship to the fullness of its meaning. . . . Right here in Montgomery, when the history books are written in the future, somebody will have to say, 'There lived a race of people, a black people, fleecy locks and black

complexion, a people who had the moral courage to stand up for their rights. And thereby they injected a new meaning into the veins of history and of civilization.'"

The first few days of the boycott gave it added momentum and provided the black community with a new sense of pride and dignity, and a spirit of working together. The boycotters walked cheerfully, sometimes in the rain, and very often for great distances. Old men and women walked as well as young children. Some rode mules through the streets or drove horse-and-wagon rigs. Others rode in one of the 210 black-operated taxicabs, whose owners had agreed to let passengers ride at bus-fare rates. New volunteer car pools were formed each day.

But they didn't ride the buses!

Soon it was obvious to the owners of the bus

company and to the white community that black people were not going to ride the buses unless their terms were met. They wanted only three things: courteous treatment from drivers; seating on a first-come, first-served basis; and the employment of black bus drivers.

The bus company and the city officials would not agree to the terms, so the boycott continued. Then the city officials began a "get tough" policy with the boycotters. Car-pool drivers were stopped and asked to show their licenses and insurance policies. On the smallest excuse, they were given tickets. Riders waiting to be picked up were threatened with arrest as hitchhikers. Most of the boycotters stood firm. Only a few quit the car pools, fearful that their licenses might be revoked or their insurance cancelled. Some quit because they were afraid that they could not remain nonviolent in the face of police abuse.

Then one day, Dr. King himself was arrested on a trumped-up charge. But he was not to be behind bars for long. News of his arrest spread quickly throughout the black community, and everyone began heading toward the jail to see what could be done to help.

Soon, such a large crowd of well-wishers was gathered outside the jail that the jailer began to panic. He released Dr. King on his own and personally ushered him out of jail.

Before long, more violent methods were used to try to force the protesters to end their boycott. Early one night, a bomb was tossed on the porch of Dr. King's home while he was at a mass meeting. Just before the bomb exploded, Coretta grabbed their infant daughter and ran to the rear of the house. Most of the front windows of the Kings' home were broken and the living room was a shambles — but Coretta and the baby were safe. Luckily Coretta had heard "something heavy drop on the front porch."

By the time Dr. King received news of the bombing and arrived at his home, an angry crowd of black supporters had gathered around his house. Police were unable to control them. Many were armed and obviously unwilling to remain nonviolent.

"If you have weapons," Dr. King said to them quietly, "take them home. If you do not have them, please do not seek to get them. We cannot solve this problem through violence. . . . Remember the words of Jesus: 'He who lives by the sword shall perish by the sword.' . . . We must meet hate with love."

Neither bombing, harassment, nor trickery stopped the boycott, and after three months, a Montgomery grand jury met and concluded that the boycott was illegal. They then proceeded to arrest ninety of the boycotters and their leaders. Cheerfully, all of them surrendered and went to jail.

Dr. King received word that there was a warrant out for his arrest while he was on a speaking tour in Nashville, Tennessee. He hurried back to Montgomery and, like the others, voluntarily gave himself up.

By now the nation's press had learned of the mass arrests, and reporters and television crews swarmed into Montgomery from all over. When March 19, the day of the trial, arrived, the press of the world covered the event. Among them were newsmen from France and England—and from India, the liberated nation whose leader, Gandhi, had inspired Martin Luther King.

After a four-day trial, Dr. King was found guilty of "violating the state's anti-boycott law." The judge then sentenced Dr. King to pay a fine of

$500 and an equal amount in court costs. Because Dr. King chose to appeal rather than pay, the sentence was converted to 386 days in prison. The defense filed a notice of appeal, the sentence was suspended, and Dr. King was released on bond.

Two months later, on May 11, a federal civil action lawsuit that the boycotters brought against the city of Montgomery and the state of Alabama was argued before three federal judges. The judges took three and a half weeks to come to a decision, but it was worth waiting for. They decided that the segregation laws governing city buses in Montgomery could not be enforced because they were unconstitutional. But total victory was not yet won.

Lawyers for the city of Montgomery now took the case to the United States Supreme Court, the highest court in the land. Once again, Montgomery lost.

On November 13, 1956, the Supreme Court also declared that Alabama's bus segregation laws were unconstitutional.

After 381 days of walking for freedom, Montgomery's black population of 50,000—with Martin Luther King Jr. as their leader—had won out against injustice. They had stood together as black Americans had never before stood together. And they had won a new dignity for themselves and the respect of the world in their victory.

WE SHALL OVERCOME

FROM THIS TIME FORWARD, there was no turning back for Dr. King. Overnight, he found himself the leader of an awakened people. Plans were made to extend protests all over the South. A new organization was formed. It was called the Southern Christian Leadership Conference (SCLC), and Dr. King was elected its president.

Other groups joined the fight for freedom. White college students from the North joined forces with black college students from the South. They banded together and began sit-ins at restaurants and stores that would not serve black people. They were met with threats and often with beatings. But they were not stopped, and they did not "lose" their nonviolence.

Then the freedom rides began. Groups of black people and white people from all over the country boarded buses in the South and sat together in the white section. They tested bus-station restaurants and highway restaurants, insisting that the black people among them had the right to be served in places of public accommodation. They were carted off to jail by the hundreds. In jail, they went on hunger strikes and sang freedom songs.

"We Shall Overcome" became the freedom fighters' song. It was sung on picket lines at bus stations and on protest marches. People joined hands at rallies in the lonesome fields of the rural South and sang it by the light of flickering torches. As they marched to jail, they sang:

We are not afraid, we are not afraid,
We are not afraid today.
Oh, deep in my heart I do believe
We shall overcome someday.

Wherever the freedom movement reached a crest, Dr. King was there to give his people courage and spiritual guidance. Older protest groups like the Urban League and the NAACP gave their support to the freedom movement. They were joined by newly formed groups like the Congress of Racial Equality (CORE) and by the Student Non-Violent Coordinating Committee (SNCC).

Clergy of all faiths joined the movement. White Episcopalian ministers were jailed for freedom riding, and rabbis fasted and prayed in the jails of the South. A Catholic bishop insisted that the white schools in his diocese admit black children.

Dr. King spoke at rallies of thousands and at small gatherings in the fields. His growing family saw very little of him, but his wife, Coretta, stood firm.

Their second child, Martin Luther King III, was only a year old when a mentally ill black woman stabbed Dr. King with a letter opener in New York City. He was in critical condition for days.

While Mrs. King was carrying Dexter Scott, their third child, Dr. King was serving time in an Atlanta jail for leading a protest march.

A few days after Mrs. King gave birth to their younger daughter, Bernice Albertine, Dr. King finished a week of demonstrations in Birmingham, Alabama. He led a crowd of 2,500 black protesters straight through police lines and headed downtown. They were arrested at lunch counters and on the streets. But they still came, rank on rank, dressed in their Sunday best and singing "We Shall Overcome."

Fire hoses were turned on them, and many were thrown to the ground by the powerful streams of water. Others took their places. All in all, 3,300 black protesters were arrested that week in Birmingham. They were carted off to jail, still singing. Among them was Dr. King.

Coretta was worried. Usually when Dr. King was jailed, he was able to get word through to her. But this time he was being held in solitary confinement. Finally, in desperation, she placed a call to President Kennedy to try to find out if her husband was all right, but she could not reach him. The threat of violence or sudden death was never far from Coretta's thoughts. Early the following evening, Coretta received a long-distance call. She picked up the phone and the operator said shortly, "Will you please get your child off the phone?"

Two-year-old Dexter had picked up the extension phone downstairs and was busily chattering away. He had no idea that he was interfering in affairs of state. The operator was trying to connect President Kennedy with Mrs. King! The president was calling to assure her that her husband was safe and that the FBI was standing by.

The Kings did not find it easy to bring up a normal family in the setting of Dr. King's work. The two older children, Yolanda and Dexter, began to ask why their father kept going to jail. They knew that people generally go to jail for doing wrong. Coretta assured them that their father went to jail "to help people." Still, other children teased them about it and there were hard moments.

Dr. King always tried to spend as many weekends as possible with his family and he did his best to never miss a holiday at home. But the freedom movement demanded more and more of his time. One year, he traveled 275,000 miles and made 350 speeches!

The freedom rides, the sit-ins, and the protest marches kept going strong. Students tramped the red dirt roads of Georgia and swamplands of Mississippi, encouraging black people to register and vote.

The surge toward freedom was answered by the burning of four black churches in Georgia. A white mailman, William Moore, walking the roads as a lone freedom marcher, was murdered in Alabama. Medgar Evers, a black leader, was shot to death on his own front porch in the dead of night in Mississippi—and there were other martyrs.

It was a time of trouble and terror but a time of triumph, too.

I HAVE A DREAM

ON AUGUST 28, 1963, a huge civil-rights demonstration, the March on Washington for Jobs and Freedom, was held. It was the largest crowd ever to gather in Washington, D.C.—over a quarter of a million strong.

Old and young, black and white, Gentile and Jew—housewives, servants, sharecroppers, singers, and statesmen—gathered around the Washington Monument. Shoulder to shoulder, they marched to the Lincoln Memorial.

They had poured into Washington by the busload. They had jammed the waiting rooms of hundreds of small train stations. Seats on planes were not to be found, and car pools inched forward, bumper to bumper, on the roads that led into Washington — from the North, South, East, and West.

Many came from overseas, too — diplomats from the African nations and press representatives from the capitals of Europe.

Weeks before the great day, an eighty-two-year-old man left Dayton, Ohio, for the march on a silver bicycle. A civil-rights worker made the trip from Chicago to Washington on roller skates.

The military police were out in full force, too. Businessmen and officials feared that violence might break out in such a huge crowd. But there was no violence. The crowd had learned the lessons of Martin Luther King too well.

He stood before them, dwarfed by the brooding statue of Abraham Lincoln, and he said: "I have a dream that one day on the red hills of Georgia the sons of former slaves and the sons of former slaveowners will be able to sit down together at the table of brotherhood . . . We will be able to speed up that day when all of God's children . . . join hands and sing in the words of the old Negro spiritual, 'Free at last! Free at last! Thank God Almighty, we are free at last!'"

The March on Washington gave the civil-rights movement new importance. Dr. King and other black leaders were asked to help draft a bill that would give black Americans equal rights. *Time* magazine chose Dr. King as the Man of the Year and used his picture on its cover. He was given several honorary degrees, including a Doctor of Laws from Yale University.

Officials who had seen the tremendous show of

strength that the march expressed began to take an interest in the civil-rights bill that President Kennedy had proposed.

But the days of wrath were not yet over. On Sunday morning, September 15, a black church, which had been used for civil-rights meetings, was bombed. Four little girls were killed as they recited their Sunday school lessons. Later that day, two black teenagers were shot and killed during an ambush.

People of goodwill everywhere were deeply shocked by the murders of these innocent children. Demands for a strong civil-rights bill came from all sides. It was feared that the black community's self-control might snap if such a bill was not soon made law.

Before he was assassinated on November 22, 1963, President Kennedy presented a civil-rights bill to Congress. The bill was passed by the House of Representatives but was held up by the Senate for many months. It was finally passed by the members of the Senate and signed by President Johnson on July 2, 1964.

With the passage of the Civil Rights Act, black Americans at last had their feet on the road toward freedom.

Martin Luther King Jr. stated his people's new position when he finished a speech by saying, "And so I close by quoting the words of an old Negro slave preacher. . . . 'Lord, we ain't what we oughtta be; we ain't what we want to be; we ain't what we goin' to be; but thank God, we ain't what we wuz.'"

THE PRIZE IS WON

ON OCTOBER 14, 1964, Martin Luther King Jr. took his place among the great men of all lands who have fought for the cause of peace. On that day, it was announced that the young black American leader had won the Nobel Peace Prize.

The prize, which was first awarded in 1901, was named in honor of its donor, Alfred Bernhard Nobel, the Swedish chemist who invented dynamite. The Peace Prize is one of six Nobel prizes given each year that worthy recipients can be found. It is awarded "without distinction of nationality."

At thirty-five, Dr. King was the youngest person ever to win the award, and the second black American. The first was Dr. Ralph J. Bunche, who won the Peace Prize for his work as a United Nations mediator in the Middle East.

Dr. King flew to Oslo, Norway, on a special chartered flight to attend the prize ceremony. With him were his wife, his father and mother, his brother and sister, and many of the civil-rights leaders who had fought side by side with him for so long. Their memories of the long years of struggle were plain to see as they stood in the great hall of Oslo University. With pride, they watched a distinguished audience of world dignitaries, including King Olaf V of Norway, rise in a standing ovation for the simple Baptist minister from Atlanta.

In his presentation speech, the chairman of the prize committee described Dr. King as "an undaunted champion of peace" and "the first person in the Western world to have shown us that a struggle can be waged without violence." He spoke of Dr. King as one "who has suffered for his faith, who has been imprisoned on many occasions, whose home has been subject to bomb attacks, whose life and the lives of his family have been threatened, and who nevertheless has never faltered."

Dr. King's rich, compelling voice easily filled the huge hall as he acknowledged the award, saying, "I accept the Nobel Prize for Peace at a moment when twenty-two million Negroes of the United States of America are engaged in a creative battle to end the long night of racial injustice. I accept this award on behalf of a civil rights movement which is moving with determination

and a majestic scorn for risk and danger to establish a reign of freedom and a rule of justice. . . .

"I come as a trustee, for in the depths of my heart I am aware that this prize is much more than an honor to me personally. . . . You honor the ground crew without whose labor and sacrifices the jet flights to freedom could never have left the earth. Most of these people will never make the headline. . . . Yet when the years have rolled past and when the blazing light of truth is focused on this marvellous age in which we live—men and women will know and children will be taught that we have a finer land, a better people, a more noble civilization—because these humble children of God were willing to suffer for righteousness' sake."

FREE AT LAST

===

WHEN DR. MARTIN LUTHER KING JR.
arrived in Memphis, Tennessee, on April 3, 1968,
he was welcomed by a crowd of two thousand supporters. Dr. King had been invited to Memphis to
lead a march on behalf of the city's garbage workers, who were striking for higher wages. The strike
had become a civil-rights cause, since more than
ninety percent of the workers were black people.

On an earlier trip to Memphis, Dr. King led a
march on behalf of the strikers that ended in violence. One person was killed, many were injured,

and there were more than two hundred arrests. The violence, created by some young Black Nationalist activists, depressed Dr. King, for it was the first time in his civil-rights career that violence had erupted. This kind of outbreak suddenly threatened his whole philosophy of nonviolence. He was faced with a terrible decision. Should he return to Memphis and try to conduct another nonviolent march or yield to the possibility of further violence? This intense indecision plagued Dr. King for several days. His first thought was to get out of Memphis and never return, but then he said, "This is no time to quit. Nothing could be more tragic than to stop at this point."

He went back to Atlanta, gathered his SCLC staff together, and made plans to lead a peaceful nonviolent march through the streets of Memphis to support the garbage workers' strike. And so it was that on Wednesday, April 3, he returned to Memphis to face the supreme test of his theory of nonviolence.

All day on Thursday, April 4, Dr. King met with his staff in room 306 of the black-owned and operated Lorraine Motel in Memphis. At the end of this trying day, Dr. King dressed for dinner and stepped out on the balcony of his motel at about 6 p.m. to join his staff, many of whom had already begun to leave for the home of the Reverend Kyles, their dinner host. Dr. King had looked forward to the dinner, anticipating the period of relaxation before going to the evening mass meeting.

Dressed in his usual public attire—black suit, a tie, and a white shirt—Dr. King leaned over the iron rail of the balcony and chatted with his aides, who were standing below in the courtyard of the motel, waiting for him.

Suddenly a shot rang out. Some said it sounded like a stick of dynamite . . . another witness reported it sounded like a firecracker . . . another thought it was an automobile accident and still others said it had the sound of a bomb. The sharp sound was unusual and unexpected.

The Reverend Ralph Abernathy, Dr. King's longtime friend and close associate, rushed out of room 306 to investigate the noise and saw the fallen King stretched out on the concrete balcony floor. Abernathy knelt down beside him and tried to speak to him, but the famed, prophetic speaker was now speechless.

An ambulance was summoned by the police and arrived about fifteen minutes later. At 7:05 p.m. at Saint Joseph's Hospital, an assistant hospital administrator called together King's tense and nervous staff and read a brief but concise statement. It said, "At seven p.m. Dr. Martin

Luther King expired in the emergency room of a gunshot wound in the neck."

April 4, 1968, was the day the voice of non-violence was silenced by an act of violence. The Peaceful Warrior was gone, and with him peace and tranquility in our cities. Violence erupted in the nation's capital, and almost simultaneously, civil disorder broke out in forty-six cities. The senseless murder of the famed American ignited an emotional bonfire across the country. Angry black people spilled into the streets of numerous cities, reacting against the assassination of Dr. King, their fallen leader. Stores were burned, cars overturned, windows smashed, rocks thrown, and people were killed and injured. Within a week, the riots brought on by the death of Dr. King had claimed thirty-nine lives. The assassination had provoked the kinds of emotions that produced an antithesis to his life—violence and death.

The president of the United States, Lyndon B. Johnson, spoke to Americans on radio and television and said, "We have been saddened by the assassination of Dr. King. I ask every citizen to reject the blind violence that has struck Dr. King, who lived by nonviolence." He later issued a proclamation:

I, Lyndon B. Johnson, President of the United States, do call upon all Americans to observe Sunday next, the seventh day of April, as a day of national mourning throughout the United States. . . . I direct that until the interment the flag of the United States shall be flown at half-staff on all buildings, grounds and naval vessels of the Federal Government in the District of Columbia and throughout the United States and its Territories and possessions.

Dr. King's body went on public view Saturday afternoon, April 6, in the Chapel of Spelman College (a part of the Atlanta University system where Dr. King had gone to college) and remained there until Monday afternoon, when it was removed and carried to Ebenezer Baptist Church, formerly co-pastored by the father-son team of Dr. Martin Luther King Sr. and Jr. There it remained until the funeral services, which were held Tuesday morning.

More than 50,000 mourners passed by—some quietly, others sobbing. Some cried aloud, and others were near collapse. Many children passed by Dr. King's body. Some were so little that they had to be lifted by their parents to see the body in the glass-covered coffin.

In the wake of Dr. King's death, the overwhelming public response was one of grief and regret. Tributes came in from everywhere. They came from black and white, rich and poor, from home and abroad, from the young and the old. His children received numerous letters of sympathy and many invitations to spend their vacations with other children. One little boy wrote, "I feel so sorry that you lost your daddy. I'll be glad to share mine with you."

While preparations for the final rites were being completed in Atlanta, dignitaries and plain people were streaming into the city by the thousands. People came from everywhere — ministers from St. Louis, brick masons from Detroit, garbage workers from Memphis, congressmen from Washington, movie stars from Hollywood, friends from foreign lands, and thousands of others.

The public service was held on the campus of Morehouse College, where Martin Luther

King received his undergraduate degree and was regarded as the most outstanding alumnus of the institution.

There were so many people on the campus and the crowd was so crushing that the services had to be shortened. A number of people became ill and several fainted. After the services, the ride to the graveside began.

The Reverend Ralph Abernathy officiated at the final service and said, "The cemetery is too small for his spirit, but we commit his body to the ground."

Mrs. King sat still and strong as she listened and watched. The children had tears in their eyes. They joined their mother in putting their hands on the coffin before it was rolled into the Georgia marble crypt. Some very simple words form the epitaph on the crypt. They are words from an old slave song that Dr. King often used to end his speeches. They probably would be his words now if he could speak them: "Free at last, Free at last, Thank God Almighty I'm Free at last."

AFTERWORD

IN 1983, the Congress of the United States set up a federal holiday commemorating the life of Martin Luther King Jr. Each year, the third Monday in January is set aside to honor Dr. King and to remember how his leadership helped to change the lives of millions of Americans. The only other American with a federal holiday in his honor is George Washington.

At the ceremony for the signing of the bill establishing the holiday, President Ronald Reagan said that Dr. King's life "symbolized what was right about America, what was noblest and best." Mrs. King urged that when remembering Dr. King we should all "make ourselves worthy to carry on his dream."

"WE SHALL OVERCOME"

Musical and Lyrical adaptation by Zilphia Horton, Frank Hamilton, Guy Carawan, and Pete Seeger. Inspired by African American Gospel Singing, members of the Food & Tobacco Workers Union, Charleston, SC, and the Southern Civil Rights Movement.

Arr. Charity Bailey

2. We are not afraid, we are not afraid,
   We are not afraid today,
   Oh, deep in my heart I do believe
   We shall overcome some day.

3. We'll walk hand in hand, we'll walk hand in hand,
   We'll walk hand in hand some day,
   Oh, deep in my heart I do believe
   We shall overcome some day.

4. The truth will make us free, the truth will make us free,
   The truth will make us free some day,
   Oh, deep in my heart I do believe
   We shall overcome some day.

5. We shall live in peace, we shall live in peace,
   We shall live in peace some day,
   Oh, deep in my heart I do believe
   We shall overcome some day.

A SHORT BIBLIOGRAPHY OF BOOKS ON BLACK PEOPLE AND THE CIVIL RIGHTS MOVEMENT

Clayton, Ed. *The SCLC Story in Words and Pictures*. Atlanta: Southern Christian Leadership Conference, 1964.

Douglass, Frederick. *Narrative of the Life of Frederick Douglass, an American Slave*. New York: Signet Classics, 2005.

Du Bois, W.E.B. *The Souls of Black Folk*. New York: Dover Publications, 1994.

Gandhi, Mahatma. *The Essential Gandhi: An Anthology of His Writings on His Life, Work, and Ideas*. Edited by Louis Fischer. New York: Vintage, 2002.

Hughes, Langston. *The Collected Poems of Langston Hughes*. Edited by Arnold Rampersad. New York: Vintage Classics, 1995.

King, Martin Luther, Jr. *The Autobiography of Martin Luther King, Jr.* Edited by Clayborne Carson. New York: Warner Books, 2001.

——. *Letter from the Birmingham Jail*. Charleston, SC: CreateSpace Independent Publishing Platform, 2016.

——. *A Testament of Hope: The Essential Writings and Speeches by Martin Luther King, Jr.* Edited by James M. Washington. New York: HarperOne, 2003.

Petry, Ann. *Harriet Tubman: Conductor on the Underground Railroad*. New York: Amistad, 2007.

Sterling, Dorothy. *Freedom Train: The Story of Harriet Tubman*. New York: Scholastic, 1954.

Thoreau, Henry David. *Civil Disobedience*. Carlisle, MA: Applewood Books, 2000.

Washington, Booker T. *Up from Slavery: An Autobiography*. Radford, VA: Wilder Publications, 2008.